Winter Weather

Practicing the ER Sound

Whitney Walker

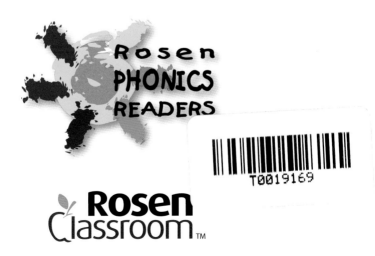

Rosen PHONICS READERS

T0019169

Rosen Classroom™

It is winter.
What is the weather like?

It snows in winter.
Winter is windy, too!

The weatherman says
it will snow.
The winter snow falls.

The snow falls faster.
My teacher sees the snow.

"It is just a snow shower,"
says Miss Baker.

The snow falls harder.
I have never seen such weather.

Miss Baker sends
everyone home.

"It will get better,"
says my father.

The snow falls lighter.

My mother shovels snow.
My sister plays in the snow.

I want snow every day!